THE MICHIGAN MEDICAL MARIJUANA CAREGIVER'S BIBLE

Roman Moya

Copyright © 2015 by Roman Moya. All rights reserved. No portion of this book, except for brief review, may be reproduced, stored in a retrieval system, or transmitted in any form or by any means – electronic, mechanical, photocopying, recording, or otherwise – without the expressed written permission of the publisher. For information contact Blueprint Publishing.

Legal Disclaimer: The information contained in this guide is for educational and research purposes only. The questions and answers provided herein are intended to provide general information only and to reflect the current status of the Michigan Medical Marihuana Act Initiated Law of 2008, Public Acts 512, 514, and 460. This information should not be construed as a legal opinion or as legal advice.

Medical Disclaimer: The following information is intended for general information purposes is not intended to provide any kind of advice, explanation, opinion, or recommendation about possible legal or medical rights, remedies, defenses, options, selection of forms or strategies. Additionally, the information provided is meant to complement, not replace, the relationship between a patient and his/her own physician.

ISBN: 0692606017
ISBN-13: 978-0692606018

DEDICATION

To the flower that blooms in the dark. To the sick, suffering, and selfless individuals who have sacrificed for the revelation of truth in science, and for the miracle medicinal cannabis plant.

To Purple Rose.

CONTENTS

	Acknowledgments	i
1	Introduction	1
2	So Why Be A Caregiver Anyway?	Pg # 2
3	Protect Yourself At All Times	Pg # 5
4	Will The State Of Michigan Protect Me?	Pg # 7
5	How Do I Start Growing Plants?	Pg # 9
6	Seeds Vs. Cuttings Vs. Clones	Pg # 10
7	Enclosed Locked Facilities	Pg # 11
8	Transporting Plants	Pg # 12
9	Blooming & Flowering	Pg # 13
10	Harvesting	Pg # 15
11	Outdoor Growing (Enclosed Locked Facilities Cont…)	Pg # 17
12	Drying & Curing	Pg# 19
13	Assisting With A Patient's Medical Use Of Marijuana	Pg# 20
14	Immunity Vs. Medical Defense	Pg# 23
15	Bona Fide Caregiver-Patient Relationships	Pg# 28
16	All Things Considered	Pg# 34
17	Frequently Asked Questions & Answers	Pg# 40
18	Outro	Pg# 50
19	Sources	Pg# 51

ACKNOWLEDGMENTS

First and foremost, I would like to say thank you to all of the wonderful patients and caregivers I have met throughout the world who have believed in the truth of the medicinal cannabis plant.

Thank you to Purple Rose. You know who you are.
I Love you for that.

Thank you to all of the wonderful people who provide support to medical marijuana patients and caregivers in Michigan including: Lila Brown, Dennis M. Hayes, Esq., Dr. Pastor Aperocho, M.D., Michael Komorn, Esq., Rep. Jeff Irwin, David Rudoi, Esq., Rick Thompson, Kevin McCaffery, Josh Jones, Esq., David Brogren, Jamie Lowell, Nick Zettel, Denise Pollicella, Esq., Magdalena Cox, Dr. Sharon Roddy, M.D., Chuck Ream, Deborah Arnold, & Vertigo.

1
INTRODUCTION

In 2008 the voters of the State of Michigan, via a voter referendum enacted law with an overwhelming 63% of the state voted Yes to giving medical marijuana patients and their caregivers special immunities from arrest and prosecution as well as special defenses in legal situations to protect their choice to engage in the medical use of marijuana.

Fact: Marijuana is illegal. Even in the state of Michigan.
Fact: Everyone involved in the Michigan Medical Marijuana Program who deals with marijuana directly is breaking the law.
Fact: Registered Michigan medical marijuana caregivers have immunity from arrest and prosecution for assisting with a registered qualifying patient's medical use of marijuana.
Fact: Immunity is Not the same as having a Right to do something.
Fact: You must assert your immunity in order to avoid arrest and prosecution.
Fact: Growing marijuana takes a lot of skill and hard work. Anyone who tells you it is easy either hasn't done it themselves or hasn't done it right.

2
SO WHY BE A CAREGIVER ANYWAY?

Caregivers are unique individuals who assist qualified medical marijuana patients with the *Medical Use* of marijuana. [01] Every caregiver has their own goals and obstacles when assisting a medical marijuana patient just as every patient has their own requirements for a caregiver.

Caregivers can receive compensation for their work. The Michigan State Supreme Court offered insight in 2011 when it ruled that caregivers could be compensated for the work that they do for a qualifying patient that they care for.[02] The ruling also gave insight to how a caregiver can qualify for certain tax deductions based on their related activities in their role as a registered caregiver.

Being a registered caregiver for a qualified medical marijuana patient can be very rewarding and those who understand that marijuana is a commodity will quickly realize the potential financial rewards that come along with cultivation as well. Be careful though, as growing marijuana does not come without its headaches (we will talk more about how to get set up the right way).

People from all walks of life are learning about the medicinal properties that marijuana has and we all have our own way of engaging in the industry. Some caregivers are breeders and are looking to create new marijuana strains, others are spouses or family members who are assisting a close loved-one with the medical use of marijuana. Some caregivers are money motivated and see this as a business opportunity while others might just be looking to help as many people as possible in a newly formed medical environment. No matter your reasons, so long as your heart is pure and your intent is to provide care then you can find a rewarding practice as a medical marijuana caregiver.

SO LET'S GET STARTED

We are going to cover some very controversial points in the next few pages so pay close attention to the words that are being used as definitions in the Michigan Medical Marihuana Act. Words are very powerful when applied to the conduct that a registered caregiver is allowed to engage in while assisting a registered patient with the medical use of marijuana.

The minimum requirements to be a registered caregiver in the state of Michigan are as follows:
- You must be a legal resident of the state of Michigan and carry a valid Michigan photo ID or equivalent in order to assert immunity under the Michigan Medical Marihuana Act.
- You must be 21 years of age or older.
- You cannot have a prior felony conviction in the past 10 years, and none that were ever relating to drugs or assault.

If you can meet those requirements then you can become a registered medical marijuana caregiver in the state of Michigan. [03]

Now that we know you can meet the requirements to be a caregiver, you must now register with the state of Michigan. In order to register as a caregiver, you will need a qualified patient willing to let you assist them with the medical use of marijuana.

Advertisement:
Are you ready to become a caregiver and need a legitimate qualified patient? The Michigan Caregiver Network can help! Visit www.MichiganCaregiverNetwork.com in order to get matched with a legitimate qualified medical marijuana patient and secure your immunity the right way.

Rule: A registered caregiver can have full immunity from arrest and prosecution for up to five (5) medical marijuana patients that they are registered to assist with the medical use of marijuana.

Strategy: Make sure that all of your patients have legitimate qualifying conditions. [03] The Michigan State Supreme Court echoed in a recent case that is important to understand as much as possible about your patient's medical use of marijuana including what qualifying condition(s) they have and how you are assisting them in the course of treating those conditions. [04] (In these particular cases the caregivers couldn't provide the courts with information supporting their immunity such as the condition the patient had, how much medicine they receive, how much medicine was necessary to grow, or even how they used the medicine)

Purpose: Your immunity as a caregiver is based on a medical defense that the registered patient has for their specific qualifying condition. So in essence your defense is only as good as the defense of the patient you are assisting. [05] Therefore, make sure you only work with legitimate qualified patients who received their certification in the course of a bona fide physician-patient relationship as defined under state law. If the patient you are registering was certified at a dispensary, grow store, 'certification shop', or any other place that the state has deemed as "medically unsound" then you will be at risk. It is always better to go to doctor's office or clinic that sub-specializes in qualifying patients for medical marijuana certification. (See First Natural Wellness' website [06] for "The Clinic" [07] in Ann Arbor or Nuit Health's office [08]) Make sure that the physician who certified your patient has a medical license free from negative marks or disciplinary actions or this could allow a prosecutor to poke holes in your defense and ultimately make it appear that you don't have immunity based on the patient not being qualified properly. These are very important steps to take initially in order to form a basis for your immunity should you ever need to assert it.

3
PROTECT YOURSELF AT ALL TIMES

As you may have heard once before in a boxing match, the same is true in the world of caregivers, you must protect yourself at all times when it comes to your dealings with your registered medical marijuana patients.

So what kind of defenses should you have in place? Once you have made an arrangement with a qualified patient to become their caregiver, the next step is to decide plant possession. Not every patient is willing to let their caregiver possess their plants. While this may seem odd, it is the choice of the patient.

Fact: Becoming a patient's registered caregiver does not automatically entitle you to plant possession. You must check the box on the patient's application or change form to indicate that you as the caregiver will keep possession of the 12 plants.

Once you have filed a patient's paperwork properly, designated yourself as a caregiver, in possession of the patient's 12 marijuana plants you then must wait to hear from the state of Michigan for approval of your immunity. The Medical Marihuana Program has 21 business days by law to issue a medical marijuana card for new/renewal patients and their caregivers. You will want to wait to hear back from the state's licensing division for the approval letter before you will have immunity to assist the patient. During this wait time, you should be able to get the necessary components in place to begin providing for your new patient.

Fact: The words 'marihuana' and 'marijuana' mean the same thing but are based on different spellings depending on where the term originated. The state of Michigan prefers to use the Polynesian way of spelling marihuana without the 'j' and in favor of the more pronounced 'h' to describe the medicine.

4
WILL THE STATE OF MICHIGAN PROTECT ME?

The short answer is no. The state has no obligation to protect you or your activities as a caregiver. You must protect yourself. Therefore, we cannot only rely on the state's marihuana program forms to indicate that you have immunity. Sometimes a separate agreement is necessary for patients and caregiver to maintain ultimate protection. The Michigan Caregiver Network has the forms, agreements, and contracts necessary for you to maintain your immunity under the MMMA at www.MichiganCaregiverNetwork.com.

In our private agreement with patients we will need to include a few components, in addition to what the state would like to know, about this arrangement. Once you and the patient have decided on plant possession and the patient is willing to let you grow their plants, you will want to keep an agreement stating what they are entitled to. Remember, the plants technically belong to the patient so in order to make sure that you receive fair compensation for your time, energy, equipment, and utilities; you will need to include these components in your arrangement. Make sure that your agreement includes a predetermined price that the patient will pay you for the medicine in grams and ounces at a minimum. The agreement should also include a term length so that the patient doesn't just "change their mind" and leave you hanging with 12 marijuana plants while they switch to a new caregiver. Safe access points are also worth discussing with your patients so that you will have a plan for assisting them with delivery or meeting somewhere safe to transfer medicine. While these are pretty basic components to include in a patient-caregiver agreement, for ultimate protection it is wise to know what qualifying condition(s) you are helping a patient find relief for and wise caregivers will also require constant feedback from their patients so they are able to document which strains, forms, and dosages are working for them. This is all proof of your immunity should you ever need to assert it.

Fact: It is not a requirement to be a patient in order to be a registered caregiver. Nor is it required to be a caregiver in order to be a qualifying patient. It is possible to be both a registered qualifying patient and registered caregiver for up to five (5) additional patients. As a patient, you could possess your own 12 plants + 2.5 ounces of usable marijuana, and 12 additional plants + 2.5 ounces of usable marijuana for each of your five (5) registered patients bringing you to a total possible possession of 72 marijuana plants and 15 usable ounces!

Fact: A caregiver and their registered patient in the same place, at the same time could possesses up to 5 ounces of usable marijuana collectively. The patient is allowed their 2.5 ounces of usable marijuana and the caregiver can hold an additional 2.5 ounces in reserve for them.

5
SO HOW DO I START GROWING PLANTS?

Caregivers have shared resources from the time the voters approved the Michigan Medical Marijuana Act in 2008. Many caregivers know someone, either a patient or caregiver, currently operating within the program that they are able to gain valuable knowledge and experience from. The Michigan Caregiver Network was created to bring those caregivers closer together. In order to start cultivating you will need a secure location with space enough to create a suitable growing environment. Some caregivers prefer to grow outdoors but are limited with seasonal weather changes. Examples of grow rooms and setup designs can be found on the internet but if you would like consulting on this topic then go to www.MichiganCaregiverNetwork.com to speak with a friendly caregiver representative who can help you get started.

6
SEEDS VS. CUTTINGS VS. CLONES

Once you have your location and environment in proper working order, the next thing you will need to do is get growing inside. Seeds can be found from many places online, or from other members in the Michigan Caregiver Network. Clones are usually 'cuttings' of a specific plant which can be used to create an entirely new plant, hence the term 'clone' or 'cloning'. Once the cutting has a root system then it can become a verifiable clone of the plant which the cutting came from. For faster results, and in order to cut a couple of weeks off your initial vegetative cycle, most growers will try to find clones, or 'teen' plants that are nearing their potential for a successful flower cycle.

Fact: Seeds do not count against your weight limits in the MMMMA. Theoretically you can have as many seeds as you want. There is no limit.

Fact: Any marijuana you produce with a root system is a plant by definition. Even if you have a seedling with a tiny little root tip pushing through the shell of the seed: That is a plant by definition. It is no longer a seed. Be very careful to stay within your allotted plant count numbers in order to have full immunity.

7
ENCLOSED LOCKED FACILITIES

In order to have full immunity the marijuana plants you possess must be kept in an enclosed, locked facility. The caregiver is the only person allowed to have access to the facility and no one else is allowed around the plants, so make sure that no one else can access the location where the plants are kept locked. Not even the patient you are growing them for is allowed in the enclosed, locked facility. Multiple enclosed, locked facilities at one address will constitute at least one illegal marijuana grow. Cohabitation growing [09] is not defensible and should be avoided. In other words, two people at the same address can not operate multiple grows. Only one person would potentially have immunity if you were both charged with a crime.

Strategy: Never use a key lock for your enclosed, locked facility when you can use a combination lock. If it can be proven that anyone other than the registered caregiver had access to the keys of the enclosed, locked facility then it could be argued that someone other than the registered caregiver had possession of the marijuana plants in which case both people could be charged with a crime without a defense. It would also be nearly impossible to prove anyone else knew the combination to the lock if no one else said they knew it.

8
TRANSPORTING PLANTS

While we are on the topic of your grow room (enclosed, locked facility) let's discuss moving plants. If you are able to acquire plants already growing or you need to move plants you currently possess then you will need to take very strict precautions. When transporting plants in a vehicle it is important that no one else is in the vehicle with you except your registered patient that you are possessing them for. It would be wise in this scenario, with or without your registered patient, to be extremely incognito when moving plants. Some growers prefer to do it in the middle of the night while their neighbors are sleeping in order to avoid detection of your grow room. Some growers will rent a small moving truck depending on the number of plants and how big they are. Most plants can fit in large moving boxes or you can use a large plastic bag to wrap over the top of them when physically moving them out of the grow room and into the vehicle used for transportation. While in a vegetative state most marijuana plants can withstand a good amount of stress so after the move they should rebound quickly if they get knocked around at all.

Strategy: If you are limited in space when transporting plants you can lay them down. In order to secure it, you can create a Styrofoam lid over the base of the pot to keep the soil contained while the plant is lying sideways.

9
BLOOMING & FLOWERING

It is our purpose here to help registered caregivers follow the rules for immunity rather than to give growing advice. We have added this section because we believe there will be a larger discussion to be had about flowering marijuana plants versus vegetating them or a combination of both as the laws for immunity are interpreted in the courts. Our advice in this section for now is simple and includes a focus on security.

The design of your grow room should include components to avoid detection and prevent intrusion. More trouble comes to caregivers who do not employ simple rules for remaining private and confidential in their affairs. You should never tell anyone you grow marijuana and never reveal the whereabouts of your secret grow location.

Fact: You are NOT required to share the address of your grow house(s) (enclosed locked facility) with anyone, even the state. When registering with the state of Michigan you will be required to give them a Mailing Address, where you can receive mail correspondence. This could be any family member's address where you can receive mail, a work address or even a PO Box. [10]

Fact: There are NO laws or rules requiring a registered caregiver to post anything on their grow room door or on any other part of the structure they are growing in. Registered caregivers are NOT required to label plants with patient names, numbers, or any other revealing information.

You can use special locks and surveillance equipment both on the inside and outside of your grow room which can be easily found at your local hardware store. And don't forget to cover up that smell with a charcoal filter or air ionizer, especially as you get closer to harvesting the medicine.

10
HARVESTING

Preparing for your harvest can be tricky depending on where you are growing and where you plan to harvest the medicine. Most patients will prefer a caregiver to trim, dry, and cure the medicine before assisting them with it in a usable form. During pre-harvest and while trimming the buds you will end up with unusable material including dried sun leaves with hardly little or no medicine on them. You will want to get rid of these leaves without anyone having access to them. Caregivers who discard their unusable material in their normal trash will have law enforcement picking through their garbage in no time. Don't be silly. Burn anything unusable so that it is never counted as usable marijuana should you ever run into legal trouble.

Fact: Under the Michigan Medical Marijuana Act, seeds, stalks, and stems of the marijuana plant are not considered usable marijuana and will not count against your weight limits. [11]

Fact: "Usable Marijuana" is defined under the MMMA as: the dried leaves and flowers of the marihuana plant, and any mixture or preparation thereof, but does not include the seeds, stalks, and roots of the plant. [12]

So there you have it, even if those leaves don't have medicine on them and you think they are just trash in the bag, based on the Usable Marijuana definition, the leaf or flower simply has to be dry to be counted against your weight, so make sure to burn them if you can.

IF I AM ONLY ALLOWED TO POSSESS 2.5 OUNCES PER PATIENT, THEN HOW CAN I HARVEST A WHOLE PLANT AT ONE TIME?

Good question and this is one that is largely unanswered. Some growers have recommended a "stutter-harvest" by where you only cut down so much of the plant at one time, but there are several complicating factors that can arise from this method so you won't find many caregivers employing such tactics. Keeping in mind that if the plant still has a root system (you haven't chopped it down from the base) then you could dry and cure the whole plant without cutting off each individual bud, but you won't find many caregivers operating this way either.

So what do you do? Well, some have argued that since "Usable Marijuana" is by definition the dried leaves and flowers then "Wet Marijuana" or that which is still fresh and filled with moisture & chlorophyll is NOT usable so it should NOT count against your weight limits. Most attorneys in the medical marijuana field will advise their clients to label marijuana that is NOT DRY OR USABLE so that it strengthens a defense for their immunity if they are ever accused of having more usable marijuana then they are allowed. [13]

11
OUTDOOR GROWING
(ENCLOSED LOCKED FACILITIES CONT...)

The rules for immunity to grow marijuana outdoors are laid out in the definitions of the enclosed, locked, facility and are stated plainly: Marihuana plants grown outdoors are considered to be in an enclosed, locked facility if they are not visible to the unaided eye from an adjacent property when viewed by an individual at ground level or from a permanent structure and are grown within a stationary structure that is enclosed on all sides, except for the base, by chain-link fencing, wooden slats, or a similar material that prevents access by the general public and that is anchored, attached, or affixed to the ground; located on land that is owned, leased, or rented by either the registered qualifying patient or a person designated through the departmental registration process as the primary caregiver for the registered qualifying patient or patients for whom the marihuana plants are grown; and equipped with functioning locks or other security devices that restrict access to only the registered qualifying patient or the registered primary caregiver who owns, leases, or rents the property on which the structure is located.

So in order to grow outside, you will need to employ many security functions including being able to restrict access to the structure the plants are being grown in. Security cameras equipped with night vision would be a huge benefit to any outdoor grower and the stakes get higher (no pun intended) when you have to deal with predators in the form of animals and thieves.

12
DRYING & CURING

From a logical design perspective, your drying and curing area should be separate from your grow room. You may want to designate a small closet or half bathroom if you have the space to begin drying the medicine for your patients. It would be wise to control any smells that might prompt curiosities from the neighbors. Again, while this medicine is NOT usable, it should be labeled as such so that it doesn't count against your medicine that is ready for your registered patient to use.

Most caregivers choose to cure their patient's medicine in mason jars. The art of 'burping' the jars is something you will become familiar with as you release odorous gasses that the medicine is releasing during this phase. The jars can also be kept in the same space you dry the medicine and with both parts of the drying & curing processes it is always better to keep the medicine in the dark, away from harmful light rays that can damage the cannabinoids on the leaves & flowers.

13
ASSISTING WITH A PATIENT'S MEDICAL USE OF MARIJUANA

A registered caregiver has immunity to transfer marijuana to their qualifying patient and a caregiver is allowed to receive compensation for assisting the patient with the medical use of marijuana. The law describes several immunities associated with the term "medical use" but, primarily a caregiver has immunity for assisting their patient with actually using marijuana (administering it), possessing & acquiring marijuana for the patient (including manufacture and cultivation), and transporting the marijuana for the patient. So long as the registered caregiver's activity was directed at assisting their qualifying patient with the medical use of marijuana, then they will always have a built-in defense for their actions with legal remedies.

The immunity for transportation of marijuana is very specific and should be adhered to with strict caution. If you are transporting marijuana as the driver of a motor vehicle then you need to keep the marijuana in the trunk of the vehicle and further in a locked case. [14] The law is very specific about this. If you are driving a vehicle without a trunk (truck, jeep, hatchback, etc) then you must keep the marijuana in a locked case not readily accessible from the interior of the vehicle. Most lawyers we have spoken with believe that if you are not the driver of the vehicle then the transportation requirements do not apply to you. In other words, if you are the passenger in a vehicle then you can have the marijuana on your person or in your baggage. The operator of the motor vehicle is under the jurisdiction of the Michigan Vehicle Code and there is no mention of how a passenger would have any liability.

Strategy: The Michigan State Police have issued 'guidance' for what they consider to be "out-of-reach" to a driver of a motor vehicle. They state that "two-steps-removed" is sufficient for something to be "out-of-reach" to the driver. In other words, it would have to take the driver two separate motions to get to the container. Always make sure you have a lock on your container and as long as it is out of reach then it will never be left open to law enforcement's interpretation as to whether you actually had access to the container from the interior.

Tip: Luggage locks are the simplest way to create a locked container. If you have a backpack or any other small piece of luggage with two zippers then you can easily create a locked container by using a luggage lock to secure the two zippers together. Remember, the best lock to use is a combination lock and luckily your local retail store will carry many different kinds for you to pick up for a low cost. Storing your medicine in smell proof bags will help you avoid any unwanted questions, search warrants, or other potential probable cause scenarios. The bags we are referring to are commonly used with food products for an air tight seal and usually come with a component that vacuum locks the package.

Theory: We have spoken with many expert attorneys in the practice of medical marijuana and they unanimously believe that the transportation amendment (MCL 750.474) to the MMMA was not codified properly to actually be able to place a "penalty" on a registered patient or caregiver that is following the rules for immunity. And while some registered patients and caregivers have been arrested because of this, there is not one case that has made its way to the Michigan State Supreme Court in order to test the theory of it being inapplicable.

There are two principal problems in judicial review under the Equal Protection Clause: The role of the courts in constitutional adjudication and the test to be applied. The questions of what role and which test are interrelated. The choice of test is frequently determinative of the judicial role. [15]

The question when and how actively a court should exercise its power of constitutional review has engendered vigorous debate. [16]

It has been said that "legislatures exist to decide the wisdom of statutes, courts exist to decide their constitutionality." [17] That the legislative solution appears undesirable, unfair, unjust or inhumane does not of itself empower a court to override the legislature and substitute its own solution. [18] A legislative classification need not be drawn with "mathematical nicety";[19] "rough accommodations illogical, it may be, and unscientific" will do. [20] Statutes are cloaked with a presumption of constitutional validity. The burden of rebutting that presumption is on the person challenging the statute.

One can accept the philosophy of judicial restraint which lies behind "rules" explicating the heavy burden that must be borne by one who assails the constitutionality of a presumptively valid and incontestably wise statute, and still recognize "the responsibility of the courts to strike the statute" where "the legislature's judgment of the wisdom of a statute is shown to conflict with a constitutional limitation on legislative power"

14
IMMUNITY VS. MEDICAL DEFENSE

Without getting too carried away here, we would like to present a few different scenarios where a caregiver may be asserting immunity versus taking a stand with a medical defense. Immunity is different than a 'Right' that someone has been given, as we have stated in the beginning of this guide.

As a registered caregiver in the State of Michigan you are entitled to immediate immunity under section 4 of the MMMA. This immediate immunity has to be asserted by presenting at the minimum a medical marijuana caregiver license and valid Michigan photo ID or equivalent.

Legal guides define immunity as follows: Legal protection from liability, obligation, or penalty. Types of immunity include (1) Criminal immunity conferred on a witness to secure vital testimony, revelation of which may otherwise incriminate the witness; (2) Judicial immunity protects a judge from implication of words or actions arising in the exercise of judicial duties, and (3) Sovereign immunity protects a government and agencies from civil (non-criminal) liability.

The immunity prescribed to caregivers under the MMMA states: A primary caregiver who has been issued and possesses a registry identification card **shall not be subject to arrest, prosecution, or** penalty in any manner, or denied any right or privilege, including but not limited to civil penalty or disciplinary action by a business or occupational or professional licensing board or bureau, for assisting a qualifying patient to whom he or she is connected through the department's registration process with the medical use of marihuana in accordance with this act. The privilege from arrest under this subsection applies only if the primary caregiver presents both his or her registry identification card and a valid driver license or government-issued identification card that bears a photographic image of the primary caregiver.

This subsection applies only if the primary caregiver possesses an amount of marihuana that does not exceed:

(1) 2.5 ounces of usable marihuana for each qualifying patient to whom he or she is connected through the department's registration process; and
(2) for each registered qualifying patient who has specified that the primary caregiver will be allowed under state law to cultivate marihuana for the qualifying patient, 12 marihuana plants kept in an enclosed, locked facility; and
(3) any incidental amount of seeds, stalks, and unusable roots.

The prescribed immunities for caregivers also states: There shall be a presumption that a qualifying patient or primary caregiver is engaged in the medical use of marihuana in accordance with this act if the qualifying patient or primary caregiver:

(1) is in possession of a registry identification card; and
(2) is in possession of an amount of marihuana that does not exceed the amount allowed under this act. The presumption may be rebutted by evidence that conduct related to marihuana was not for the purpose of alleviating the qualifying patient's debilitating medical condition or symptoms associated with the debilitating medical condition, in accordance with this act.
(e) A registered primary caregiver may receive compensation for costs associated with assisting a registered qualifying patient in the medical use of marihuana. Any such compensation shall not constitute the sale of controlled substances.

So wait, what did they just say?

The law is protecting a registered caregiver behavior and conduct with **Immunity** related to assisting their patient with the medical use of marijuana so long as the caregiver is following the *rules for immunity* which have been *italicized*.

Immunity has to be asserted. We will repeat that sentence for good measure. Immunity has to be asserted. Since you are actually breaking the law (manufacture, possession, distribution of marijuana, etc) if you are ever confronted by law enforcement then you will need to prove you have immunity to engage in the activities related to your duties as a caregiver.

Please keep in mind that you have an obligation to your patient upon initiating yourself as their caregiver to keep their personal medical information private. Persons (even caregivers) guilty of violating HIPAA can be punished with a misdemeanor and up to a $10,000 fine for revealing personal health information that they are privy to about someone who wishes it to remain private and confidential.

The Michigan Medical Marijuana Act (MMMA) was passed by voters of the state of Michigan in 2008. Since most of the immunities you have available to you are relatively new to law enforcement sometimes it is necessary to educate them if they are unfamiliar with the law. (Did anyone just hear the music stop?)

Hold up, so cops might not know the law or realize you have immunity?

Yes!, it's true. Law enforcement has not had proper training to deal with medical marijuana patients and caregivers so most of them do not even understand the law or how you have immunity.

Keep in mind, most veteran law enforcements officers are used to throwing people in jail just for the smell of marijuana so for them to adjust, to have to now think about letting someone go, even if that person has marijuana on them, is very hard for certain police officers to understand, let alone cope with.

Tip: Always keep a copy of the Michigan Medical Marijuana Act wherever you have medical marijuana so you have the ability to help educate law enforcement if the time arises to do so.

Law enforcement can also lie to you and it is perfectly legal for them to do that in order to coerce you into giving them information they believe would be useful to prove a crime is being committed. Sometimes it can be tricky to know if a member of law enforcement is lying to you or whether they just don't understand the law. If they are unsure then they will try to arrest you just to see if they were right in their opinion of enforcing the law. Remember, it is not a police officer's job to interpret the law. They are simply meant to enforce the law.

Tip: In Michigan it is completely legal to record any conversations or video that you are party to. Never hesitate to whip out that camera phone and record a police officer in order to prevent them from operating outside of their command.

If we recall from the previous listed prescribed caregiver immunities the law states: there shall be a presumption that a qualifying patient or primary caregiver is engaged in the medical use of marihuana in accordance with this act if certain conditions are met which relate to assisting the patient with the medical use of marijuana. In that same section it also states: *The presumption may be rebutted by evidence that conduct related to marihuana was not for the purpose of alleviating the qualifying patient's debilitating medical condition or symptoms associated with the debilitating medical condition, in accordance with this act.*

So the only way for a law enforcement officer to deny you your immunity would be to prove that you were not following the rules for immunity. How can they do that? They have to have evidence that you are not following the rules for immunity. Let's say you had a bag of marijuana sitting in your passenger seat during a routine traffic stop. You may show the officer your medical marijuana license to assert immediate immunity but they can rebut you claim for immunity by proving you are illegally transporting the marijuana by not properly keeping it in the trunk and further in a locked container.

Caregivers must take special precautions to ensure that they are covering all of their bases with respect to the immunity they are being granted which relies entirely on the patient's ability to demonstrate their need for medical marijuana.

Strategy: On your medical marijuana license you will be assigned a registry number which starts with the letter "C" and is followed by two consecutive 6-digit numbers for example: C111222-333444. That is the only number that law enforcement would need to use to confirm with your photo ID that you are entitled to immunity. You must still present the medical marijuana card in order to assert immunity but some caregivers feel more secure by taking black electrical tape and covering up all of the other information except the registry number. Technically all of the other information being revealed on the medical marijuana card is protected under health laws and should not be revealed to just anyone, including an officer of the law who is not entitled to personal health information in order for you to assert immunity. Some caregivers will even instruct their patients to cover up all of their personal information on the back of the card to keep their anonymity.

If you are arrested and charged with a crime pertaining to the medical use of marijuana you still have an opportunity to have your case dismissed. In order to do this you will need to mount a section 8 defense. This can be nearly impossible if you don't have a strong enough relationship with your patient. Because a section 8 defense can be complicated we will start our discussion in the next section based on what we like to call the Bona Fide Caregiver-Patient Relationship.

15
BONA FIDE CAREGIVER-PATIENT RELATIONSHIPS

While the law does not explicitly state that you need to have a deep understanding of your patient's medical use of marijuana the courts in this state have echoed it loud and clear. If you are ever put into a legal defense position you will need to know intimate details about your registered patient's medical use of marijuana.

In the Michigan court case of *People v. Hartwick* we get a glimpse into how the court system will allow a medical defense for a caregiver by understanding what the court wanted from Hartwick in addition to just his medical marijuana card (Hartwick doesn't seem to 'get it'):

Defendant (Hartwick) was charged with manufacturing and possession with intent to deliver and he moved to dismiss the charges, under Sections 4 and 8 of the MMMA.

At an evidentiary hearing, the defendant testified that he was a medical marijuana patient and a caregiver for five additional medical marijuana patients. The defendant introduced registry identification cards for himself and his five patients.

While the cards confirmed the defendant's status as a caregiver, the defendant "was unfamiliar with the health background of his patients and could not identify the maladies or 'debilitating conditions' suffered by two of his patients."

Furthermore, the defendant "was not aware of how much marijuana any of his patients were supposed to use to treat their respective conditions or for how long his patients were supposed to use 'medical marijuana.' And he could not name each patient's certifying physician."

In regard to the defendant's Section 8 defense, the prosecution argued that "defendant did not know the amount of marijuana necessary to treat his patients' debilitating medical conditions, meaning that defendant could not meet the evidentiary requirements of the section 8 affirmative defense."

In response, the defendant (Hartwick) argued that the patient and caregiver registry identification cards were all that he needed "to establish the fact that these people were authorized by the state of Michigan and approved."

The trial court held that the defendant was not entitled to assert the Section 8 defense at trial.

The court reasoned that "it heard no testimony regarding a 'bona fide physician-patient relationship or a likelihood of receiving therapeutic or palliative benefit from the medical use of marijuana,' or any testimony on whether defendant possessed no more marijuana than reasonably necessary for medical use."

On appeal, the defendant argued that "mere possession of [a registry identification card] entitles him to ... an affirmative defense under section 8."

A panel of this Court rejected that argument, explaining, "a registry identification card is necessary, but not sufficient, to comply with the MMMA but clearly does not satisfy the section 8 requirements for a total defense to a charge of violation of this act."

This Court proceeded to hold that proof of a registry card standing alone could not satisfy the first element of a Section 8 defense. This Court reasoned that a bona fide physician-patient relationship is a "pre-existing and ongoing relationship with the patient as a treating physician," and that "[a] registry identification card ... cannot demonstrate a 'pre-existing relationship between a physician and a patient, much less show 'ongoing' contact between the two."

Apart from the registry cards, the defendant failed to present any other evidence to support the first element of a Section 8 defense: here, defendant presented evidence of a bona fide physician-patient relationship between him and his doctor. But he presented no evidence that his patients have bona fide physician-patient relationships with their certifying physicians. None of [the defendant's] patients testified. Nor was defendant able to provide the names of his patents' certifying physicians.

The plain language of section 8 obviously requires such information for a patient or caregiver to effectively assert the section 8 defense in a court of law.

With respect to the second element—i.e. the patient or caregiver possessed only an amount of marijuana that was "reasonably necessary to ensure uninterrupted availability"— this Court explained that this element "involves two components: (1) possession, and (2) knowledge of what amount of marijuana is 'reasonable necessary' for the patient's treatment."

These requirements necessitate "a patient or caregiver that is intimately aware of exactly how much marijuana is required to treat a patient's condition, which he learns from a doctor with whom the patient has an ongoing relationship."

This Court concluded that the defendant failed to offer evidence to support the second element, stating: Here, defendant lacks the requisite knowledge of how much marijuana is required to treat his patients' conditions—and even his own condition.

He presented no evidence regarding how much marijuana he required to treat his pain and how often it should be treated. And he testified that he did not know how much marijuana his patients required to treat their conditions. Defendant thus failed to satisfy the second element of the section 8 affirmative defense.

Given that the defendant failed to create questions of fact as to the first and second elements, and considering that the trial court did not make findings with respect to the third element, this Court did not address whether the defendant's testimony satisfied the third element.

Instead, this Court again explained that mere possession of a patient or caregiver registry card was insufficient to support the third element of a Section 8 defense.

So in order to present a proper section 8 defense, the court is saying that three elements must be presented for you to have your charges dismissed:

1. The caregiver's patient can demonstrate maintaining a bona fide physician-patient relationship.
2. The caregiver has a bona fide relationship with their patient and possesses an amount of marijuana that is sufficient for the uninterrupted supply for the patient's required use.
3. The caregiver was engaging in the medical use of marijuana to treat or alleviate their patient's qualifying condition(s).

So what constitutes a bona fide patient-caregiver relationship?

The court interpretations of cases involving a section 8 marijuana defense tell us that there is no limit to how much you can know about your patient's medical use of marijuana. If you are working with a qualifying patient or scouting new patients then they must be willing to share vital pieces of personal information with you from the beginning in order for you to assert your defense should the need ever arise. Do not work with a patient who is not willing to give you the information you need to defend yourself.

Based on our experience, we believe caregivers should especially gather certain pieces of information from their patients during the initial time of registering them with the state and prior to the assistance with the medical use of marijuana.

Caregivers should obtain the following from their patients:
- Any and all copies of the patients medical marijuana application and/or change form designating you as the registered caregiver.

- Any copies of cashed checks or money orders paid to the state of Michigan.
- Any correspondence from the state of Michigan including approval letters and denials letters.
- Any medical records, including physician certification that the patient has used to qualify for a medical marijuana card to ensure that they have established and are maintaining a bona fide physician-patient relationship.
- A contract which may include at the minimum how much marijuana the patient needs daily, weekly, monthly, etc. Some patients may not know their dosage so it may be wise to overestimate this number in the event they do require higher doses after building up a tolerance. Other patients might prefer different forms of medicine so the dosage may be different based on how they are consuming it.
- A signed health care release form giving the caregiver direct access to the patient's certifying physician who qualified them for the medical use of marijuana.

If you are missing one thing off that list then you easily limit your abilities to assert a medical defense for assisting your patient with the medical use of marijuana.

STARTING A CAREGIVER-PATIENT RELATIONSHIP:

When initiating a relationship with a patient to be their caregiver it is important to set expectations and build your relationship on trust. Some things that may need to be worked out at first are:

- Has the patient actually been certified legitimately in the course of a bona fide physician-patient relationship?
- The quantity of medicine they will need, and how often.
- The specific strains and forms they are looking for to treat or alleviate their condition(s).
- How long it will take you to produce what they are looking for you to grow.
- Your compensation requirements.
- Scheduling and arranging for the delivery of the medicine, as well as where to meet.

And while these are just a few examples of the steps to take before becoming a patient's caregiver it is also wise to take into account their ethical and moral character. Is this patient going to become a problem legally? Do they follow the rules for immunity? Would they do something to put you at risk? These are all questions to ask yourself before moving forward with becoming a patient's registered caregiver. Remember, your immunities and defenses as a registered caregiver depend on your patient's ability to prove that they are following the law too.

MAINTAINING YOUR CAREGIVER-PATIENT RELATIONSHIP

Each patient you care for may have their own health challenges that they are looking for you to assist them with. In order to strengthen your defense we suggest keeping a log of your patients, how much medicine they use in as many different frequencies and dosage intervals as possible, which strains may be working better for certain ailments, and any updates from their physician's follow up that can help you understand the patient's medical condition(s).

It is important to communicate with your patient(s) regularly in order to know which medical marijuana treatments are effective. You will want to check back after 24-48 hours of providing them with medicine to know if there were any adverse side effects or if there were any positives. Working with your patient to effectively monitor and gauge their outcomes after using the medicine will best keep you protected and ensure you are maintaining a healthy caregiver-patient relationship.

Strategy: When dealing with multiple patients it is important to pay attention to when your caregiver card will expire so you can remind your patient when their renewal period is coming up. Presently, the State of Michigan will allow a patient and caregiver to renew their licenses within 60 days from the expiration date on the card. Because some patients may be heavily medicated or even bedridden it's best practice for the caregiver to pay attention to when the cards are expiring.

16
ALL THINGS CONSIDERED

When all things are considered with respect to the current state of affairs of the Michigan Medical Marijuana Program, really it's a convoluted mess. We have tried to make this as easy to understand as possible, but the realities are such that everything will boil down to a case by case scenario where you must be able to mount a defense related to your activities as a medical marijuana caregiver. Here we will consider some situations based on actual cases.

August, 2012
John Ter Beek vs. City of Wyoming, Michigan

In this declaratory judgment action, plaintiff, John Ter Beek, appeals as of right the trial court's order granting summary disposition in favor of defendant, City of Wyoming. Plaintiff sought to void defendant's zoning ordinance on state preemption grounds because the zoning ordinance was enacted to prohibit conduct permitted by the Michigan Medical Marihuana Act (MMMA), MCL 333.26421 et seq. Because we conclude that defendant's zoning ordinance directly conflicts with the MMMA, and the federal Controlled Substances Act (CSA), 21 USC 801 et seq., does not preempt section MCL 333.26424(a) of the MMMA, we reverse and remand.

Our Interpretation: *No local governing body, i.e. municipality, township, or city can trump the state law which provides* *patients & caregivers immunity for the medical use of marijuana. In this case the City of Wyoming tried to create a local ordinance that prevented John Ter Beek from having immunity under the MMMA for growing his own marijuana plants in his own home. They messed with the wrong guy. John Ter Beek is an attorney. He challenged the City of Wyoming and WON!*

December, 2012
People of The State of Michigan vs. Bylsma

Ryan M. Bylsma, a registered primary caregiver under the Michigan Medical Marihuana Act (MMMA), MCL 333.26421 et seq., was charged in the Kent Circuit Court with manufacturing marijuana in violation of MCL 333.7401(1) and (2)(d). Defendant moved to dismiss the charge, asserting that as the registered primary caregiver of two registered qualifying patients, he was allowed to possess 24 marijuana plants and that the remainder of the 88 plants seized by the police from his leased unit in a building belonged to other registered primary caregivers and registered qualifying patients whom defendant had offered to assist in growing and cultivating the plants. The court, George S. Buth, J., denied the motion, holding that the MMMA contains the strict requirement that each set of 12 plants permitted under the MMMA to meet the needs of a specific qualifying patient must be kept in an enclosed, locked facility that can only be accessed by one person, that defendant had failed to comply with that requirement, and that defendant was therefore not entitled to invoke either the immunity provided by section 4(b) of the MMMA, MCL 333.26424(b), or the affirmative defense contained in section 8 of the MMMA, MCL 333.26428.

Defendant appealed by leave granted. The Court of Appeals, GLEICHER, P.J., and HOEKSTRA and STEPHENS, JJ., affirmed, holding that defendant was not entitled to section 4 immunity because the MMMA did not authorize him to possess the marijuana plants that were being grown and cultivated for registered qualifying patients whom he was not connected to through the Michigan Department of Community Health (MDCH) registration process and that his failure to meet the requirements of section 4 immunity made him ineligible to raise the section 8 defense.

Our Interpretation: *This is a simple matter of possessing too many plants. Bylsma tried to say that the other plants were actually those of other registered patients and caregivers but they were found at his address. So even if they were someone else's who lived there with him he would still be in violation of the MMMA and left without any protections. Therefore, "collective growing" or cohabitative growing will not provide you with immunity or a medical defense under the Michigan Medical Marijuana Act.*

February, 2013
State of Michigan vs. McQueen

In the Brandon McQueen case the State of Michigan was attempting to shut down Compassionate Apothecary, LLC which was operated by McQueen as a caregiver along with his partner, Matthew Taylor who was also a registered caregiver. While the state was successful in closing their dispensary with the oldest trick in legal history, the public nuisance law, the Michigan Supreme Court's ruling included several insights worth noting:

1. Section 3(e) of the act, MCL 333.26423(e), defines "medical use" broadly to include the transfer of marijuana to treat or alleviate a registered qualifying patient's debilitating medical condition or symptoms associated with the debilitating medical condition. Because a transfer is any mode of disposing of or parting with an asset or an interest in an asset, including the payment of money, the word "transfer," as part of the statutory definition of "medical use," also includes sales. **Our Interpretation:** *Caregivers are allowed to receive compensation for providing their registered patients with marijuana.*

2. MCL 333.26424(d) creates a presumption of medical use and then states how that presumption may be rebutted. A rebutted presumption of medical use renders immunity under § 4 of the MMMA inapplicable. Under the statute, the presumption may be

rebutted upon a showing that the conduct related to marijuana was not for the purpose of alleviating the qualifying patient's debilitating medical condition or symptoms associated with the medical condition in accordance with the act. **Our Interpretation:** ***Patients and caregivers are automatically presumed to be complying with the michigan medical marijuana act unless there is evidence to prove otherwise.***

3. Section 4(i) of the MMMA, MCL 333.26424(i), permits any person to assist a registered qualifying patient with using or administering marijuana, but the terms "using" and "administering" are limited to conduct involving the actual ingestion of marijuana. Section 4(i) did not apply to defendants' actions, which involved assisting patients with acquiring and transferring marijuana. **Our Interpretation: Any person, even a caregiver has the right to a defense for actually helping a patient consume or apply marijuana for medical purposes.**

July, 2015
People of The State of Michigan vs. Hartwick & Tuttle

Since this case is very lengthy and contains multiple defendants we will extract some relevant information that applies to caregivers.

Robert Tuttle was charged in the Oakland Circuit Court with three counts of delivering marijuana, one count of manufacturing marijuana, one count of possessing marijuana with the intent to deliver it, and two counts of possession of a firearm during the commission of a felony. Tuttle was a registered qualifying patient under the MMMA who served as his own primary caregiver. It was unclear whether he was properly connected as the primary caregiver to one or two other registered qualifying patients. Tuttle was arrested for selling marijuana on three occasions to an individual with whom Tuttle was not properly connected under the MMMA.
Tuttle claimed immunity under section 4 and the affirmative defense under section 8 of the MMMA. The trial court, Michael D. Warren, Jr., rejected both claims and denied Tuttle's request to present a section 8 defense at trial. According to the court, immunity was not

appropriate because Tuttle's illegal conduct —selling marijuana to an individual outside the protection of the MMMA — tainted Tuttle's conduct with regard to the other charges. The trial court denied Tuttle use of the affirmative defense in section 8 because Tuttle failed to present prima facie evidence of each element of the defense. The Court of Appeals denied Tuttle's application for leave to appeal. In lieu of granting Tuttle's application for leave to appeal, the Supreme Court remanded the case to the Court of Appeals for consideration as on leave granted.

In a unanimous opinion by Justice ZAHRA, the Supreme Court held: The availability of immunity under section 4 of the MMMA is a question of law to be decided before trial, and a defendant has the burden of proving by a preponderance of the evidence his or her entitlement to immunity. Immunity must be claimed for each charged offense, and the burden of proving immunity is separate and distinct for each offense. Conduct that is noncompliant with the MMMA with respect to one charged offense does not automatically rebut the presumption of medical use with respect to conduct relating to any other charged offenses. Rather, noncompliant conduct involved in one charged offense can negate otherwise compliant conduct involved in a separate charged offense if there is a nexus between the noncompliant and the otherwise compliant conduct. Raising an affirmative defense under section 8 of the MMMA requires a caregiver to present prima facie evidence of each element of the defense for him - or herself and for each registered qualifying patient to which the caregiver is connected. Having established a prima facie case, the defendant has the burden of proving each element by a preponderance of the evidence. A valid registry identification card does not create any presumption for purposes of section 8.

Our Interpretation: The Supreme Court is speaking very clearly about the rules for immunity and the proper procedure for asserting a section 8 defense. They are saying that a registered patient or caregiver can assert their medical defense but each charge must be argued individually and even if one of the charges sticks, it does not mean that person can't bring about another defense for separate charges that may have to do with related conduct. The Michigan Supreme Court is also saying

that simply having a medical marijuana card does not entitle you to a section 8 defense. As we stated in a previous chapter, your section 8 defense will hinge on your patient's ability to show that they have followed the rules for immunity.

Fact: Possession of a firearm while in possession of marijuana is illegal and may put your case under a federal jurisdiction where you will have NO opportunity to present immunity or a medical defense.

There are several important legal cases that have shaped the interpretations of how caregivers and patients have immunity and are able to assert a medical defense in court. We must pay close attention to anytime the Michigan State Supreme Court makes a ruling on a case as it tell us what the judicial branch is thinking when they decipher who is entitled to protections under the MMMA and how they have protections to engage in the medical use of marijuana.

The Michigan Caregiver Network works with the best attorneys in Michigan who represent the healthcare, criminal defense, and marijuana fields. Feel free to contact us in order to get a referral. You can also visit the website to review attorney listings at www.MichiganCaregiverNetwork.com

So when all things are considered here in Michigan with the medical marijuana program, you will need to do the following at the very minimum when engaging in the medical use of marijuana: Arm yourself with the knowledge of how to operate within the rules of immunity, Find a trusted legal advisor (a good attorney), and Keep up with the court's rulings on medical marijuana cases to ensure you are always up to date with how the judicial system will either grant you immunity or allow you to assert a medical defense.

17
FREQUESNTLY ASKED QUESTIONS

For the entire year of 2015 the Michigan Medical Marijuana Program, which is administered by the Licensing And Regulatory Affairs (LARA) division of the State of Michigan, decided that they were going to remove the frequently asked questions page on their website. We feel that LARA either felt compelled to remove the FAQ to avoid any legal involvement in pending judicial matters or they did not want to provide guidance to the medical marijuana community to help ensure their safety. No matter what their reason was for removing it, we made sure to retain a copy. In this section we will extract some of LARA's answers to common questions about the medical marijuana program and share some of our own answers to questions posed to the Michigan Caregiver Network's members.

Question: What changes did Public Act 460 create to the Michigan Medical Marihuana Act?

LARA Answer: Public Act 460 went into effective December 27, 2012. This amendment explains the transportation of usable marihuana in or upon a motor vehicle or any self-propelled vehicle designed for land travel.

Question: What changes does Public Act 512 create to the Michigan Medical Marihuana Act?

LARA Answer: Public Act 512 goes into effective April 1, 2013. This amendment defines a "Bona fide physician- patient relationship", and further defines "Enclosed, locked facility," "Primary caregiver," and "Written certification."

Public Act 512 also expands Section 4 of the Michigan Medical Marihuana Act to provide for the privilege from arrest only if the qualifying patient or caregiver presents both his or her registry ID card and a valid driver license or government issued ID card.

Question: How are the laws and rules of the MMMA enforced?

LARA Answer: The MMP enforces the registration process making sure applications are complete before issuing a registry ID card, making incomplete or fraudulent applications null & void, and revoking cards if individuals commit violations of the MMMA. The MMP verifies the validity of a registration card of patients and caregivers with local and state law enforcement personnel if they call the MMP requesting such information. Local and state law enforcement personnel may take any action they believe is necessary to enforce the criminal laws of the state, including violations of the MMMA. Local and state law enforcement actions may vary. The MMP has no authority to direct the activities of local and state law enforcement agencies.

Question: How can I open a dispensary?

LARA Answer: This is not addressed in the MMMA, therefore; the MMP is not authorized to provide information regarding this issue.

Question: How do I know if I am eligible to be a caregiver?
LARA Answer: The MMMA defines a "Primary Caregiver" as a person who is at least 21 years old and who has agreed to assist with a patient's medical use of marihuana and who has never been convicted of a felony involving illegal drugs.

Effective April 1, 2013, in addition to the above, any person designated as a caregiver must meet the following criteria:

A person who has not been convicted of any felony within the past 10 years or a felony that is an assaultive crime (listed below) or as defined in section 9a of chapter X of the code of criminal procedure, 1927 PA 175, MCL 770.9a.

A person cannot be designated as a caregiver if they have been convicted of any felony within the past 10 years, have been convicted of a felony involving illegal drugs, or have a felony that is an assaultive crime as defined in section 9a of chapter X of the code of criminal procedure, 1927 PA 175, MCL 770.9a

- Threats/assault against employee of Family Independence Agency
- Assault with intent to do great bodily harm less than murder; assault by strangulation or suffocation
- Leading, taking, carrying away, decoying, or enticing away child under 14
- Kidnapping/Prisoner taking person as hostage
- Assault with intent to rob and steal; armed or unarmed
- Larceny of money or other property
- Stalking or aggravated stalking
- Assault with intent to commit felony not otherwise punished
- Terrorism; Violation of the Michigan Anti-Terrorism Act
- Use or possession of dangerous weapon
- Felonious Assault Assault with intent to maim
- Attempted murder, 1st degree murder, or 2nd degree murder
- Assault with intent to commit murder
- Assault with intent to commit CSC, or CSC 1st, 2nd, 3rd, or 4th degree
- Felonious Use of Explosives
- Manslaughter
- Mayhem
- Carjacking

- Conduct proscribed under MCL750.81 to 750.89 as felony; intent to commit conduct against a pregnant individual in order to cause or which leads to a miscarriage or stillbirth, or other harm to the embryo or fetus

Question: What other changes in the amendments will affect caregivers?

LARA Answer: Public Act 460 went into effective December 27, 2012. This amendment explains the transportation of usable marihuana in or upon a motor vehicle or any self-propelled vehicle designed for land travel.

Public Act 512 goes into effective April 1, 2013. This amendment further defines "Enclosed, locked facility." Public Act 512 also expands Section 4 of the Michigan Medical Marihuana Act to provide for the privilege from arrest only if the qualifying patient or caregiver presents both his or her registry ID card and a valid driver license or government issued ID card.

Public Act 514 goes into effective April 1, 2013. This amendment requires proof of Michigan residency (copy of a valid state driver license, copy of a valid state ID, or copy of a valid state voter registration) with the patient's application or renewal application.

Question: What if I have just been charged with a felony, but not convicted yet?

LARA Answer: It is the responsibility of the caregiver to prove they are eligible at the time the MMP receives a patient's application. If a background check reveals the caregiver has a pending felony case, they will be deemed ineligible and required to provide "true" or "certified" proof of the current status or disposition of the case. The caregiver will be deemed ineligible and required to provide updated proof each time they are designated by a patient while the case remains "pending" within the caregiver's background record.

Question: How do I become a caregiver?

LARA Answer: The Michigan Medical Marihuana Registry application is for a qualifying patient who has a debilitating condition specified in the Medical Marihuana Act. A qualifying patient can designate a primary caregiver on their application to help administer and/or grow the marihuana plants.

Therefore, an individual must first find a qualifying patient who would like help to either administer and/or grow the marihuana plants for them. (Please note: Our program is confidential and we are not authorized to provide the names of registered qualifying patients.) The individual will then complete a Caregiver Attestation and give the Attestation, along with a copy (front and back) of his/her valid photo ID (and voter registration, if necessary) to be submitted with the patient's application or renewal application.

If the qualifying patient has already submitted an application or renewal application, the patient would submit a change form (with the above documents) to add the primary caregiver.

Question: I have not received my new driver license yet. Can I provide a copy of my expired license to my patient?

LARA Answer: All documents must be currently valid when received at the MMP.
MCN Answer: From our experience LARA does not recognize postmark dates when reviewing your application. They require all documentation to be valid upon review, not when you sent it to them.

Question: What do I do if the address on my photo ID does not match the mailing address
provided on the application?

LARA Answer: The MMP does not require the address on the photo ID to match the address included on the application, provided it is a correct mailing address located in Michigan.

Question: Do I have to be a resident in the state of Michigan?

LARA Answer: Effective April 1, 2013, anyone registering with the MMP must provide proof of Michigan residency. Proof of legal residency shall be considered a copy of a valid, lawfully obtained Michigan driver license, copy of a valid official Michigan personal identification card, or a copy of a valid Michigan voter registration. A caregiver will provide this to the patient that is designating them on their application or change form.

Question: Is there a separate application fee for the caregiver?

LARA Answer: No. The fee for an application, renewal application, or change form remains the same regardless if there is a caregiver designated by the patient.

Question: How much marihuana can I possess as a caregiver?

LARA Answer: A primary caregiver who has been issued and possesses a registry ID card may possess an amount of marihuana that does not exceed 2.5 ounces of usable marihuana for each qualifying patient to whom he or she is designated by the patient; and for each registered qualifying patient who has specified that the primary caregiver will be allowed to possess his or her marihuana plants, 12 marihuana plants kept in an enclosed, locked facility; and any incidental amount of seeds, stalks, and unusable roots.

Question: How many patients can I grow/cultivate for as a caregiver?

LARA Answer: A primary caregiver is allowed up to five (5) patients at any time with a limit of 12 plants per patient.

Question: Can I be a qualifying patient and a primary caregiver?

LARA Answer: Yes. A person can be a qualifying patient and be designated as a caregiver for five (5) patients, therefore; allowed to grow up to a maximum of 72 plants total (if designated by each of the patients to possess the plants).

Question: Can I charge my patients for the marihuana and the medicinal assistance I am providing them?

LARA Answer: Section 4(e) of the MMMA states, "A registered primary caregiver may receive compensation for costs associated with assisting a registered qualifying patient in the medical use of marihuana. Any such compensation shall not constitute the sale of controlled substances."

The amount of compensation agreed upon is between the patient and the caregiver. The MMP is not authorized to intervene. If there is a disagreement you cannot resolve, you should seek legal counsel.

Question: Will I receive a registry card for each qualifying patient that designates me as their caregiver?

LARA Answer: Yes. A caregiver will receive a separate registry ID card for each qualifying patient who designates them, provided they are eligible and approved as a primary caregiver.

Question: When will my registry ID card expire for my patients?

LARA Answer: The caregiver's registry ID card will expire on the same day as each of his/her patient's registry ID card(s).

Question: Does my patient(s) have to notify me if they change to a new caregiver?

LARA Answer: When the MMP processes a change form to remove a caregiver, the caregiver will receive a notice that their registry ID card for that patient is no longer valid. Prior to receipt of the letter (which can take up to 60 days to receive) the responsibility falls on the patient to communicate with the caregiver to notify him or her that he or she is no longer protected under the law.

Question: Why is my photo not on my registry ID card?

LARA Answer: The MMP is not inserting patient/caregiver photos on the registry ID cards at this time. Law enforcement is aware of this and shall consider any MMP registry ID card with a photo to be fraudulent.

Question: What if my registry ID card is lost, stolen, or damaged?

LARA Answer: If there are any changes that need to be made to your registration you will need to submit a change form. Otherwise, submit a signed statement attesting that your registry ID card has been lost, stolen, or damaged (whichever applies) and requesting a replacement card. Specify if this is your patient card. If this is your caregiver card(s), you must include the name(s) of the patient(s) for whom you need replacement card(s). Include a copy (front and back) of your valid photo identification, and $10.00 (per card replacement) check or money order made payable to "State of Michigan-MMMP." Mail the statement, photo ID, and fee to:
Michigan Department of Licensing and Regulatory Affairs
Medical Marihuana Registry
PO Box 30083
Lansing, MI 48909

Question: If a qualifying patient designates me as their caregiver and I am approved, can I use marihuana?

LARA Answer: Not as a designated caregiver. You would have to be registered as a patient to qualify to use medicinal marihuana.

Question: Can I contact the MMP to get information on my registration?

LARA Answer: Due to the confidentiality in the law, MMP staff can only speak with the patient regarding that patient's registration or the caregiver regarding that caregiver's registration. Staff will ask for confidential details to prove your identity and will be happy to assist you.

Question: Are concentrated forms of marijuana such as hash, wax, oil, tincture, butter, etc., protected by the MMMA?

MCN Answer: Technically, no. Patients and caregivers only have protections for "usable marijuana" which means the dried leaves and flowers of the marihuana plant, and any mixture or preparation thereof, but does not include the seeds, stalks, and roots of the plant. In 2013 the appeals court decision (People v Carruthers) ruled that edible forms of marijuana made with THC extract were not covered by Section 4 immunity. If the concentrate is made with actual marijuana plant leaves or flowers it would be protected as "usable marihuana" under Section 4 so long as it contained a mixture of some form of the dried leaves. A concentrate would not be considered "usable marihuana" if it is made using THC that has been extracted from any part of the marijuana plant, void of any of the plant material. Likewise any oil or ointments made with THC extract would not be protected under Section 4's immunity. However, the medical use defense of Section 8 would allow a person who is charged with a marijuana related crime to argue that the edible or oil was for medical use and thus the criminal charges should be dismissed. Of course, presenting a Section 8 argument can be very difficult, as it requires that certain elements be met, including whether the doctor-patient relationship was bona fide, the amount of marihuana concentrate possessed, and if it was possessed for medical usage.

Question: What if someone from law enforcement wants to see my grow room?

MCN Answer: Under no circumstances do you have to let ANYONE in your grow room without a search warrant. The law states clearly that the caregiver is to maintain the grow room as an enclosed, locked facility that only they have access to.

Question: Do I have to open my door for someone without a warrant?

MCN Answer: There is no law that we know of in the entire United States of America that requires you to answer your door for anyone. If law enforcement has a warrant, then they will kick in your door without many questions being asked of you. If Johnny Law does come knocking though, it would be wise NOT to talk to them, NOT to answer your door for them, and RECORD everything they do on your property. If they are snooping or trespassing without a warrant it could prevent them from asserting their case against you and you may have the opportunity to SUE THEM.

Question: Do I have to grow marijuana plants where I live at my primary residence?

MCN Answer: No. LARA only requires a mailing address and not an address where the plants are kept. You do not have to disclose the location of your grow room to anyone. You must still maintain the plants in an enclosed, locked facility located in Michigan that only you have access to.

Question: If the property where my grow room is located happens to be in a school zone does that prevent me from growing there?

MCN Answer: No. While the federal government and the State of Michigan both have laws on the books prohibiting narcotic use, manufacture, and distribution within school zones (1000ft, 500ft respectively) the MMMA still provides immunity and a medical defense that can be asserted to allow your conduct in these areas so long as you are following the rules of immunity.

18
OUTRO

This should all sound like music to your ears if you were listening to your inner voice while absorbing all of this information. And while there are many more topics to cover and several different strategies you can employ in order to be a successful, protected caregiver, we will have to wait for more clarification on the law either by legislative action or judicial outcomes.

As this first edition is being written we have several pending court cases and decisions that will be made over the next several weeks. We also have three separate bills that have a good chance at becoming law in the near future. Those three bills will create immunities for patients and caregivers who deal with concentrated forms of marijuana as well as the addition of a tiered licensing platform similar to the liquor control commission that will license dispensaries or provisioning centers as they are called in the bills.

Anyone who purchases this book or receives a copy by joining the Michigan Caregiver Network will be entitled to new revisions for life. In order to receive revisions we will need to hear from you. Please send an email to booklist@michigancaregivernetwork.com and we will make sure that you are provided with updated information regarding any changes to the MMMA that will affect your caregiver status.

Sources:

[01] "Medical use" means the acquisition, possession, cultivation, manufacture, use, internal possession, delivery, transfer, or transportation of marihuana or paraphernalia relating to the administration of marihuana to treat or alleviate a registered qualifying patient's debilitating medical condition or symptoms associated with the debilitating medical condition.
[02] State of Michigan v McQueen - http://courts.mi.gov/Courts/MichiganSupremeCourt/oral-arguments/2012-2013-arguments/Pages/143824.aspx
[03] "Qualifying Condition" or "Debilitating medical condition" means 1 or more of the following:
(1) Cancer, glaucoma, positive status for human immunodeficiency virus, acquired immune deficiency syndrome, hepatitis C, amyotrophic lateral sclerosis, Crohn's disease, agitation of Alzheimer's disease, nail patella, or the treatment of these conditions.
(2) A chronic or debilitating disease or medical condition or its treatment that produces 1 or more of the following: cachexia or wasting syndrome; severe and chronic pain; severe nausea; seizures, including but not limited to those characteristic of epilepsy; or severe and persistent muscle spasms, including but not limited to those characteristic of multiple sclerosis.
(3) Any other medical condition or its treatment approved by the department.
(4) To date, only PTSD has been added as a new condition.
[04] People of the State of Michigan v Hartwick (Richard) http://courts.mi.gov/Courts/MichiganSupremeCourt/oral-arguments/2014-2015/Pages/148444.aspx
[05] People of the State of Michigan v Hartwick (Richard) http://courts.mi.gov/Courts/MichiganSupremeCourt/oral-arguments/2014-2015/Pages/148444.aspx
[06] First Natural Wellness – "Michigan's Most Trusted Certifications" http://www.FirstNaturalWellness.com
[07] Nuit Health, Inc DBA The Clinic – "Providing Bona Fide Physician-Patient Relationships" - http://www.NuitHealth.org
[08] Nuit Health – A Non-profit Health Center http://www.NuitHealth.org

[09] People of the State of Michigan v Bylsma (Ryan) http://courts.mi.gov/Courts/MichiganSupremeCourt/oral-arguments/2012-2013-arguments/Pages/144120.aspx
[10] Department of Licensing and Regulatory Affairs (LARA) Bureau of Professional Licensing - Michigan Medical Marihuana Program http://w3.lara.state.mi.us/orr/Files/AdminCode/1303_2013-105LR_AdminCode.pdf
[11] Michigan Medical Marijuana Act (2008) 333.26423 Section 3(k) http://legislature.mi.gov/doc.aspx?mcl-333-26423
[12] Michigan Medical Marijuana Act (2008) 333.26423 Section 3(k) http://legislature.mi.gov/doc.aspx?mcl-333-26423
[13] http://www.michigan.gov/mmp
[14] http://law.justia.com/cases/michigan/supreme-court/1975/54961-2.html.
[15] Bickel, The Least Dangerous Branch (Bobbs-Merrill Co, Inc, 1962); Wright, Professor Bickel, The Scholarly Tradition and The Supreme Court, 84 Harv L Rev 769 (1971); Linde, Judges, Critics and the Realist Tradition, 82 Yale L J 227 (1972); Shaman, The Rule of Reasonableness in Constitutional Adjudication: Toward the End of Irresponsible Judicial Review and the Establishment of a Viable Theory of the Equal Protection Clause, 2 Hastings Const LQ 153, 174 (1975).
[16] Keasling v Thompson, fn 4 supra, 700 (dissent).
[17] Dandridge v Williams, 397 US 471; 90 S Ct 1153; 25 L Ed 2d 491 (1970).
[18] Lindsley v Natural Carbonic Gas Co, 220 US 61, 78; 31 S Ct 337, 340; 55 L Ed 369, 377 (1911).
[19] Metropolis Theatre Co v Chicago, 228 US 61, 69-70; 33 S Ct 441, 443; 57 L Ed 730, 734 (1913).
[20] Keasling v Thompson, fn 4 supra, 700.

ABOUT THE AUTHOR

Roman Moya was born in Ann Arbor, the first city in America to decriminalize marijuana. He has been involved in the Medical Marijuana Movement since September 27, 2004 when he openly challenged Senator Jeff Sessions to a debate about repealing the ban on federal financial aid for drug offenders. He lives in Ann Arbor and can be seen around the city bringing about awareness for social improvements and fostering community outreach. Roman is the co-founder of First Natural Wellness, serves as a director on the board of Nuit Health, Inc., is president of the Michigan Caregiver Network, and is a member of Cannabis Patients United.

www.ingramcontent.com/pod-product-compliance
Lightning Source LLC
Chambersburg PA
CBHW050114170426
43198CB00014B/2580